THE SUN
OUR NEAREST STAR

by Franklyn M. Branley
illustrated by Edward Miller

HarperCollins*Publishers*

To Sophia Zucker—E. M.

The art in this book was created using the computer.

The *Let's-Read-and-Find-Out Science* book series was originated by Dr. Franklyn M. Branley, Astronomer Emeritus and former Chairman of the American Museum–Hayden Planetarium, and was formerly co-edited by him and Dr. Roma Gans, Professor Emeritus of Childhood Education, Teachers College, Columbia University. Text and illustrations for each of the books in the series are checked for accuracy by an expert in the relevant field. For more information about Let's-Read-and-Find-Out Science books, write to HarperCollins Children's Books, 195 Broadway, New York, NY 10007, or visit our website at www.letsreadandfindout.com

HarperCollins®, 🔥®, and Let's Read-and-Find-Out Science® are trademarks of HarperCollins Publishers Inc.

The Sun: *Our Nearest Star*
Text copyright © 1961, 1988, 2002 by Franklyn M. Branley
Illustrations copyright © 2002 by Edward Miller III
Manufactured in The United States of America. All rights reserved.

Library of Congress Cataloging-in-Publication Data
Branley, Franklyn Mansfield, date
    The sun, our nearest star / by Franklyn M. Branley ; illustrated by Edward Miller.
        p.   cm. (Let's-read-and-find-out science. Stage 2)
    Summary: Describes the sun and how it provides the light and energy which allow plant and animal life to exist on the earth.
    ISBN 0-06-028534-6 — ISBN 0-06-028535-4 (lib. bdg.) — ISBN 0-06-445202-6 (pbk.)
    1. Sun—Juvenile literature.   [1. Sun.]   I. Miller, Edward, 1964– ill.   II. Title.   III. Series.
    QB521.5.B7   2002   2001024951
    523.7—dc21

17 18 19 20 OPM 23 22   ❖   Revised and Newly Illustrated Edition

THE SUN

OUR NEAREST STAR

At night you can see a lot of stars because the sky is dark.

When the sky is bright, you can also see a star. It is the sun. The sun is our daytime star. It is also the star closest to us.

The sun is very big. It is much bigger than Earth. The sun is almost a million miles across. If Earth was the size of a pea, the sun would be the size of a beach ball.

The sun is very far away from us. It is much farther than the moon. A spaceship takes three days to reach the moon. It would take more than three years to reach the sun.

93,000,000 miles

Moon

240,000 miles

Earth

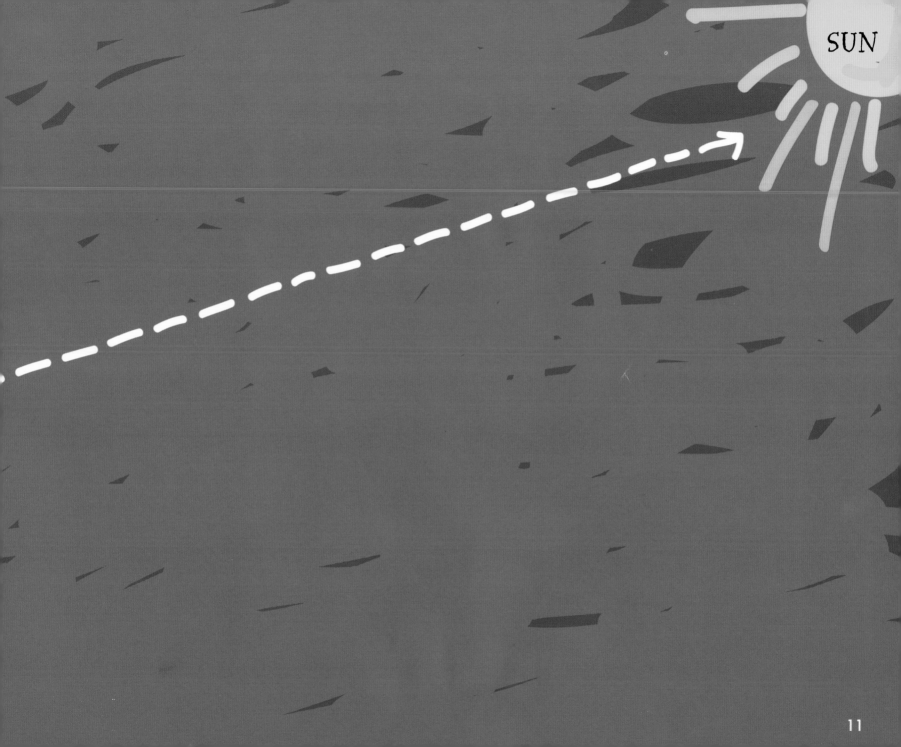

And, you remember, the sun is our nearest star. It takes eight minutes for light to travel from our daytime star to Earth. It takes four years for light from the nearest nighttime star to reach us. Most of the stars are much farther away than that.

8 minutes

SUN

Earth

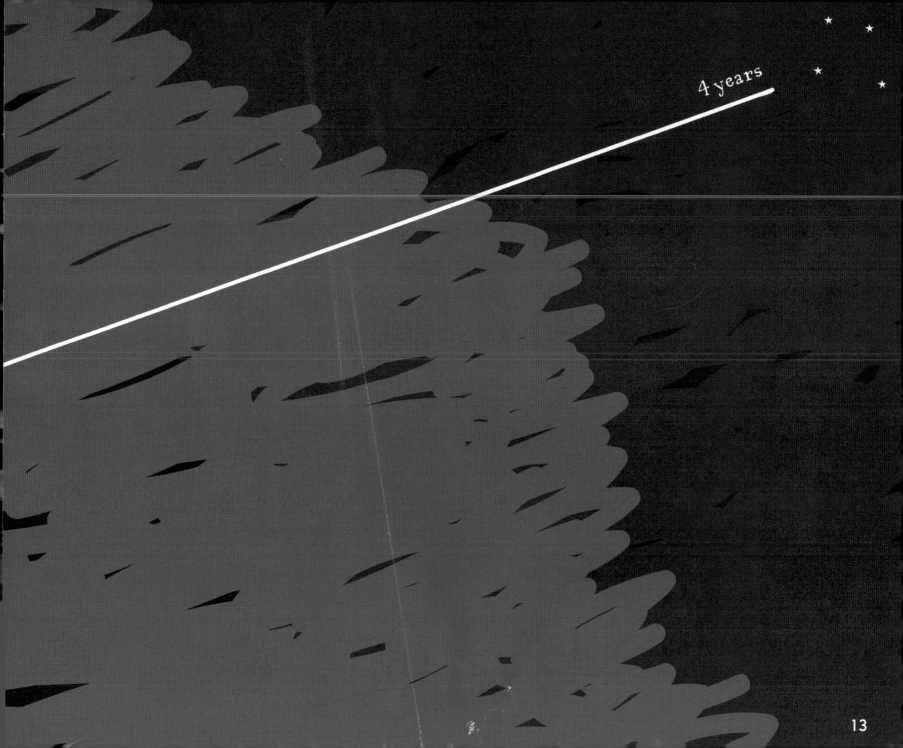

4 years

Stars are made of hot gases. In the sun and other stars there is iron, gold, copper, and tin. They are not solid as they are on Earth. All of them are gases because they are so hot.

The temperature on the surface of the sun is more than 10,000 degrees Fahrenheit. The temperature in a very hot oven is only 500 degrees.

The sun is so hot that a spaceship could not get close to it. If it ever did, the spaceship would change to gases.

10,000°F

17

The sun keeps us alive. It makes corn grow, and apples, wheat, and bananas. Animals eat the plants. We eat the plants and animals. They give us energy.

So, the energy in our food comes from the sun. It is solar energy.

Millions of years ago, Earth was covered with swamps and jungles. As plants and animals grew, they stored solar energy. When they died, they slowly changed to coal and oil. So, ancient solar energy is stored in coal and oil.

Today, we use the stored-up solar energy in coal, oil, and gasoline (which is made from oil) to fuel our cars and trucks, airplanes and rockets.

GASOL

For millions of years, the sun has warmed our planet.
It still does. It will keep shining bright and warm for
many more millions of years.

FIND OUT MORE ABOUT THE SUN

You can do a simple experiment to prove that the sun helps things grow.

All you will need are the following things:
- 2 paper cups
- some potting soil (You can buy this at any hardware or garden store.)
- a few beans (Any kind will do.)
- water

1. Fill the paper cups about halfway with soil.
2. Plant four beans in each cup.
3. Cover the beans with a little more soil.
4. Put one cup in a sunny spot, like a windowsill.
5. Put the other cup in a dark place, like a cupboard or closet.
6. Put just a bit of water into each cup, enough to dampen the soil.

After about a week, the beans will begin to sprout. Those in the sunlight will grow well. At first, those in the dark will also grow well.

Continue to water the sprouts for three or four weeks, or even longer. A spoonful of water every four days is enough. Watch for the differences between the plant in the sun and the one in the dark.

As Earth moves around the sun, the shadows that the sun casts change position. You can use these shadows to tell time. The kind of clock made by the sun and a shadow is called a sundial.

All you need are the following materials:
- a long stick
- a small square piece of clay (about 1 inch square)
- a flowerpot or a sturdy cardboard paper plate

1. Mount the stick securely in the piece of clay, and place it inside the flowerpot or in the middle of the paper plate.
2. Place the plate or flowerpot in a place where the sun will shine on it all day.
3. At the very beginning of each hour on the clock, mark the position of the stick's shadow on the pot or the paper plate using a grease pencil, crayon, or pen. Write the hour next to each mark.
4. The resulting marks around the inside edge of the pot or plate will resemble those on a clock! Now you will be able to tell the time, using just your sundial.

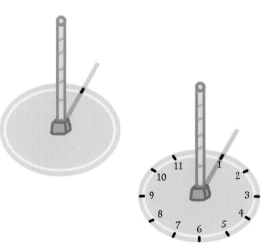